Science That's Appropriate <u>and</u> Doable

This science resource book was written with two goals in mind:

- to provide "good" science for your students
- to make it easy for you

What makes this book "good" science?

When you follow the step-by-step lessons in this book, you'll be using an instructional model that makes science education relevant to real life.

- Your students will be drawn in by interesting activities that encourage them to express what they already know about a concept.

- Your students will participate in hands-on discovery experiences and be guided to describe the experiences in their own words. Together, you'll record the experiences in both class and individual logbooks.

- You'll provide explanations and vocabulary that will help your students accurately explain what they have experienced.

- Your students will have opportunities to apply their new understandings to new situations.

What makes this book easy for you?

- The step-by-step activities are easy to understand and have illustrations where it's important.

- The resources you need are at your fingertips — record sheets; logbook forms; and other reproducibles such as minibooks, task cards, picture cards, and pages to make into overhead transparencies.

- Each science concept is presented in a self-contained section. You can decide to do the entire book or pick only those sections that enhance your own curriculum.

For sites on the World Wide Web that supplement the material in this resource book, go to http://www.evan-moor.com and look for the <u>Product Updates</u> link on the main page.

Using Logbooks as Learning Tools

Logbooks are valuable learning tools for several reasons:
- Logbooks give students an opportunity to put what they are learning into their own words.
- Putting ideas into words is an important step in internalizing new information. Whether spoken or written, this experience allows students to synthesize their thinking.
- Explaining and describing experiences help students make connections between several concepts and ideas.
- Logbook entries allow the teacher to catch misunderstandings right away and then reteach.
- Logbooks are a useful reference for students and a record of what has been learned.

Two Types of Logbooks

The Class Logbook

A class logbook is completed by the teacher and the class together. The teacher records student experiences and helps students make sense of their observations. The class logbook is a working document. You will return to it often for a review of what has been learned. As new information is acquired, make additions and corrections to the logbook.

Individual Science Logbooks

Individual students process their own understanding of investigations by writing their own responses in their own logbooks. Two types of logbook pages are provided in this unit.

1. Open-ended logbook pages:
   Pages 4 and 5 provide two choices of pages that can be used to respond to activities in the unit. At times you may wish students to write in their own logbooks and then share their ideas as the class logbook entry is made. After the class logbook has been completed, allow students to revise and add information to their own logbooks. At other times you may wish students to copy the class logbook entry into their own logbooks.

2. Specific logbook pages:
   You will find record forms or activity sheets following many activities that can be added to each student's logbook.

At the conclusion of the unit, reproduce a copy of the logbook cover on page 3 for each student. Students can then organize both types of pages and staple them with the cover.

_____'s

Plant Log

Plants • EMC 858

Name _____

This is what I learned about plants today:

Note: Reproduce this form for students to record information from daily science lessons.

Name _____

Investigation: _____

What we did:

_____

_____

_____

What we saw:

_____

_____

_____

What we learned:

_____

_____

_____

CONCEPT

A plant is a living thing.

A Search for Living Things

• Show students several objects (a plant, a small animal such as a hamster or a bird, a rock, and a book for example). Ask students to identify what is alike and what is different about the objects. List their observations.

Ask, "Can you put things together that are alike in some way?" When this has been done, ask "Why did you put these together?"

> I put the rock, the hamster, and the book together because they are brown.
>
> The book and the plant go together because they are both big and the other things are little.
>
> I put the plant and the bird together because they are alive.

• Reproduce page 9. Students are to color two or three things that go together and then write about their selection.

Discuss Their Responses

Say, "Some of you put the plant and the mouse together because they are alive. Can you name other things that are alive?"

• Divide the class into groups. Send each group to a different area in and around the school to see what living things they can find. Assign someone in each group to record their observations. (A cross-grade helper or volunteer may need to assist.)

• Have each group share their observations with the class. Record the items on the chalkboard. After the list is complete, ask students to tell why they think these items are alive. (At this point you will record all the items they name. Corrections will be made later.)

Living Things

- *bees*
- *grass*
- *ants*
- *blue jay*
- *cat*
- *oak tree*

       Plants • EMC 858

Your Class Plant Log

Begin a class plant log. Add the title "Living Things" to a sheet of chart paper. This log entry will be a definition of living things. Ask students to tell the ways they know something is alive. List these on the chart paper. Explain that they have written a meaning for living things and that this meaning is called a definition.

Characteristics of Living Things

• Gather living and nonliving items or pictures of such. Make sure a number of the items are plants. Show them one at a time.

Drawing on what was learned in the last lesson, have students give reasons why an item is living or not living. Use careful questioning to bring out characteristics that may have been omitted from the previous definition. (Living things can move, need food and water, breathe, and reproduce.) Be sure students understand that plants are alive and do each of the things in their definition.

• Have students help you correct the definition of living things in the class logbook. (All living things can move, need food and water, grow, breathe, and reproduce.)

• Reproduce page 10 for the students to complete.

• Draw a large Venn diagram on butcher paper. Use it to compare a living and a nonliving object such as a plant and a rock. Complete it as a class and then have students complete the checklist on page 11.

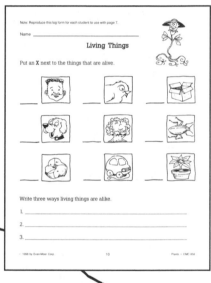

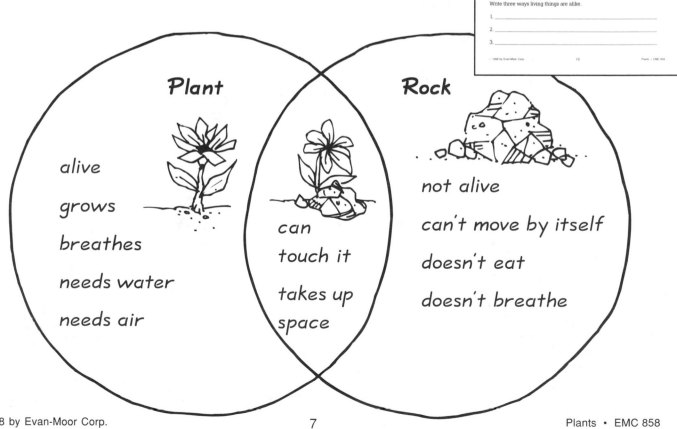

Plant

alive

grows

breathes

needs water

needs air

can

touch it

takes up

space

Rock

not alive

can't move by itself

doesn't eat

doesn't breathe

Do Plants Move?

To introduce this experiment, say to the class, "We've learned that plants are living things. One thing that living things can do is move. Do plants move?"

Do the following investigation to verify that the answer is "yes." (It is difficult for many students to accept the fact that plants move since they don't see quick movements as they do when observing animals or people.) As students observe the plants, they will see the blossom and leaves turn in the direction of the sun and leaves open and close in response to light and dark.

Materials

The plants you use will depend on what is available in your area at the time you do this activity. If those listed are unavailable, discuss other options with nursery personnel.

- sunflower plant
- prayer plant
- shamrock plant
- ivy plant

Steps to Follow

1. Set each plant in a sunny window. Have students observe the position of the blossoms and leaves. Have students check periodically to see if the leaves and blossoms have moved. Ask students to explain what they see. (*Plants turn to face the sun.*)

2. Put the prayer plant and shamrock plant in a dark area. Observe what happens. (*Plants close their leaves in the dark.*)

3. Observe how the ivy twines around its support. (*Vines wind around things.*)

4. Students write in their individual logs explaining what they know about plant movement.

 Plants • EMC 858

Name _____

These Go Together

Color two or three things that go together.

I put these together because _____

_____

_____

_____

Note: Reproduce this log form for each student to use with page 7.

Name _____

Living Things

Put an **X** next to the things that are alive.

Write three ways living things are alike.

1. _____

2. _____

3. _____

Name _____

Living or Not Living

Write **yes** in the box if it is true.
Write **no** in the box if it is not true.

	living	not living
1. I take up space.	yes	yes
2. I can move.		
3. I need food and water.		
4. I can be touched.		
5. My size can change.		
6. I grow.		
7. I have weight.		
8. I breathe.		
9. I reproduce.		

Draw one living thing.

Draw one thing that is not alive.

Plants • EMC 858

Plants have many parts.

Looking at Flowering Plants

Display several different flowering plants. Ask, "What are these? How do you know they are plants? What parts do the plants have?" Record student comments in the class logbook on a chart entitled "Plant Parts."

Divide the class into pairs or small groups. Give each group a small flowering plant and the following materials. (Give each group a different type of plant so that the class can see that all flowering plants have the same parts — roots, stems, leaves, and flowers.)

Plant Parts

Plants have
- *leaves*
- *stems*
- *flowers*
- *roots*

Materials

- a small plant in flower (buy cell packs at a garden center)
- a soft paintbrush
- several sheets of newspaper
- record sheet on page 14, reproduced for each student

Steps to Follow

1. Gently remove the plant from the pot and lay it on the newspaper.
2. Carefully brush away as much of the soil as possible.
3. Identify the parts. (Record the parts they discover on the chalkboard.)
4. Complete the record sheet by drawing the plant and labeling the parts.

Follow-up

Show a sample of each type of plant used in the investigation. Have students name the parts. Ask, "What do all of these plants have?" Have them check their record sheets to see if any corrections are needed.

Add any new information about flowering plants to the class logbook "Plant Parts." Have students list plant parts in their individual logs.

Plants • EMC 858

Looking at Trees

Go outside and observe a tree. Use questioning to help students define a tree as a plant with the same parts as the smaller plants they have been studying. (Try to find a tree where some of the roots are exposed. If none is available, explain that even though they can't be seen, trees have roots.)

Have students observe and describe ways in which a tree is different than other plants (*taller; one hard, wooden stem that is covered in bark, etc.*).

Then have students complete the tree form on page 15.

Add new understandings to a class and individual log entry entitled "Trees."

Trees
Trees are plants.
Trees have leaves.
Trees have roots.
Trees have a trunk.
A trunk is the tree's stem.

Extension Activity

Continue the study of plant parts by making collections of flowers, leaves, bark rubbings, and seeds. Place these in scrapbooks along with the plant names and where they were found.

         Plants • EMC 858

Note: Reproduce this page for each student to use with page 12.

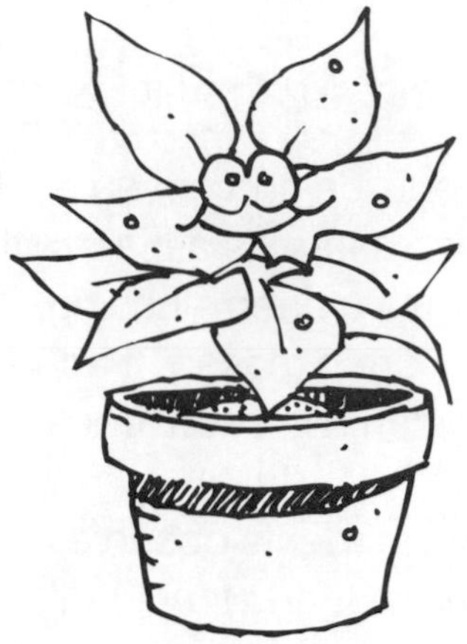

Name ______________________________

Parts of a Plant

Draw your plant in the box.
Label these parts:

root stem leaf flower

What I learned:

____

____

____

____

Name _____

Trees

Label the tree.

roots   trunk   branch   leaf   fruit

1. The stem of a tree is called

    a _____.

2. The outside cover on a

    tree is called _____.

3. A tree is different from a
    flower in these ways:

a. _____

    _____

b. _____

    _____

c. _____

    _____

Each part of a plant has a special function.

Before beginning this section, reproduce pages 26 and 27 and prepare a "Plant Jobs" booklet for each student. Directions for use of each page of the booklet accompany the lessons on pages 16–20.

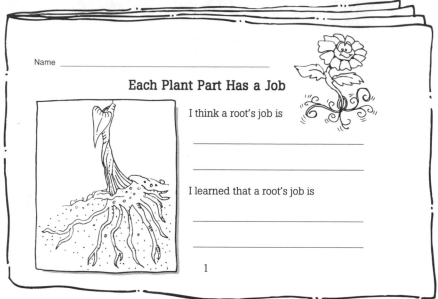

Name _____

Each Plant Part Has a Job

I think a root's job is

_____

_____

I learned that a root's job is

_____

_____

1

What Do Roots Do?

Divide students into small groups to investigate the function of roots as collectors of water for the plant.

Question students about the importance of roots to the plant. Ask, "What might happen to a plant if it lost its roots? Why?"

Have them complete the "I think" section of page 1 in their "Plant Jobs" booklets.

Materials for Each Group

- two small plants (labeled 1 and 2)
- scissors
- water
- record sheet on page 22, reproduced for each student

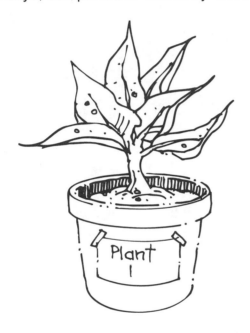

Steps to Follow

1. Remove plant 2 from its pot and shake all the soil off the roots.
2. Cut the roots off plant 2. Repot it.
3. Complete the "First Day" section of the record sheet.
4. Set both plants in a sunny location. Water as needed.
5. Observe the plants each day to see what changes occur.
6. After 10 days, complete the "Last Day" section of the record sheet.

Follow-Up

- Discuss the results of the experiment. Ask students to explain what they observed and why they think it happened. Correct any misconceptions at this point. Be sure the students clearly understand that roots are needed to collect water.

  Ask, "Can you think of any other job a root might have?" (*It holds the plant in the ground.*)

- Begin a class logbook page entitled "Each Plant Part Has a Job." Record the job of a root in the class logbook. Have the students complete the "I learned" section of page 1 in their "Plant Jobs" booklets.

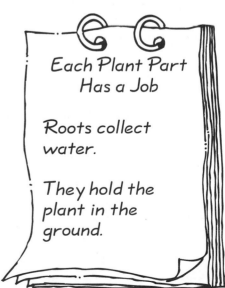

Each Plant Part Has a Job

Roots collect water.

They hold the plant in the ground.

What Do Stems Do?

This investigation will help students discover the function of stems as carriers of water for the plant.

Ask students to explain the job of stems in a plant. Have them record their thoughts on the drawing and "I think" section of page 2 in their "Plant Jobs" booklets.

Materials

- 2 glasses of water
- food coloring
- a fresh piece of celery with its top
- a white carnation
- knife (for adult use only)
- record sheet on page 23, reproduced for each student

Steps to Follow

1. Add a few drops of food coloring to the water in each glass.
2. Put the celery in one glass and the carnation in the other glass.
3. Draw the plants on the record sheet.
4. Set the glasses in the sunlight. Leave them overnight.
5. Observe the plants. Color the changes on the record sheet.
6. Cut across each stem. (This should be done by an adult.) Find the tubes that carry water up the stem.
7. Complete the written part of the record sheet.

Follow-Up

- Discuss the results of the experiment. Ask students to explain what they observed and why they think it happened. Correct any misconceptions at this point.

- After they see that stems carry water, explain that they also carry food from the leaves to other parts of the plant. Ask students to look at the plant and see if they can name another job of stems (*hold the plant up*). Add the jobs of stems to the "Each Plant Part Has a Job" page of the class logbook. Have students complete the "I learned" section of page 2 in their "Plant Jobs" booklets.

Each Plant Part Has a Job

Roots collect water.

They hold the plant in the ground.

Stems carry water.

They help hold up the plant.

How Do Plants Get Food?

• Say, "We know that living things need food to grow. How do you think a plant gets its food?" (Depending on the prior knowledge of your students, you may get answers such as: "The farmer feeds them." "Food comes from the water." "It comes from the ground.")

Say, "Every part of a plant has a job. What part do you think could make the plant food? How do you think this happens?"

• Have students record their thoughts on the drawing and "I think" section of page 3 in their "Plant Jobs" booklets.

• Because it is impossible for students to observe directly the production of food by the plant, read appropriate parts from *Straight from the Bear's Mouth: the Story of Photosynthesis* by Bill Ross (Atheneum Books for Young Readers, 1995) to help them understand the importance of the leaves to a plant.

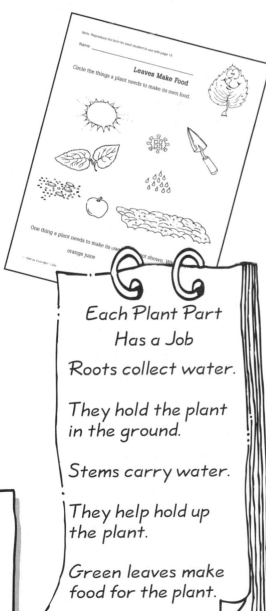

Ask students to explain what they learned from the story. Ask, "Why does the plant need the green part (chlorophyll)? What else does a green leaf need in order to make food for the plant?" Correct any misconceptions at this point.

• Record the job of leaves on the "Each Plant Part Has a Job" page of the class logbook. Have the students complete the "I learned" part of page 3 in the "Plant Jobs" booklet.

• Reproduce page 24 for each student. They are to circle all of the things a plant needs to make food.

• Add the job of leaves to the "Each Plant Part Has a Job" page of the class logbook.

Teach more able students the "formula" for making plant food.

green leaves + air + water + sunlight = plant food
or
chlorophyll + carbon dioxide + water + sunlight = sugar

Each Plant Part Has a Job

Roots collect water.

They hold the plant in the ground.

Stems carry water.

They help hold up the plant.

Green leaves make food for the plant.

What Do Flowers Do?

This investigation is to discover the purpose of flowers on a plant.

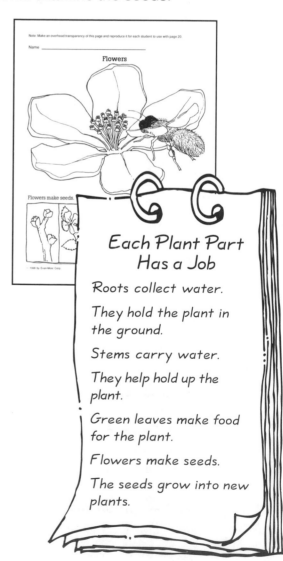

• Use a bouquet of common flowers to stimulate a discussion of flowers and their function. Guide the discussion with questions such as:

> "All of these (point to bouquet) have one name.
>   What are they called?" (*flowers*)
> "Can you name some kinds of flowers?"
>   (List these on the chalkboard.)

• Have students complete the "I think" part of page 4 in the "Plant Jobs" booklet.

• Read *The Reason for a Flower* by Ruth Heller (Grosset & Dunlap, 1983). Ask students to explain what they learned about the job of flowers.

• If possible, bring in a sunflower with seeds or a vegetable such as squash that has begun to form fruit but still contains part of the blossom. Have students examine the seeds.

• Make an overhead transparency of page 25. Also reproduce a copy of page 25 for each student. Use the transparency to review pollination and the function of a flower with your students.

Help students identify the location of pollen. Point to various parts of the flower and ask, "Do you see the pollen here?" Also point to the bee and ask students to locate the pollen (*on hind legs*).

Explain that creatures that carry pollen between flowers are called pollinators. See how many other types of pollinators they can recall from *The Reason for a Flower*. Ask them to color the pollen on the flower and on the bee.

Use the steps at the bottom of the transparency to follow the flower through its changes into a piece of fruit. Have students circle the seeds inside the fruit.

• Record the reason for a flower on the "Each Plant Part Has a Job" page of the class logbook. Have the students complete the "I learned" part of page 4 in the "Plant Jobs" booklet.

Each Plant Part Has a Job

Roots collect water.

They hold the plant in the ground.

Stems carry water.

They help hold up the plant.

Green leaves make food for the plant.

Flowers make seeds.

The seeds grow into new plants.

Plants • EMC 858

Summary Activities

Which Part Do We Eat?

Bring in a basket of fresh fruits and vegetables. (Include something for each plant part — root, stem, flower, leaf, seed, and fruit.)

Explain that plants can store food in various parts. Ask students to sort the fruits and vegetables into sets according to the part that has stored food. Have them name each set.

fruit

roots

leaves

Bulletin Board

Divide a bulletin board into sections. Label each section — roots, stems, flowers, leaves, seeds, and fruit. Divide students into six groups. Assign each group one plant part. Have students in the group draw or cut out examples of foods appropriate to their plant part. Provide books, catalogs, and magazines for reference as students plan their illustrations.

Slice up the fruits and vegetables for students to nibble as they complete their art work and pin it to the bulletin board.

Plant Parts Minibook

Reproduce the "Flowering Plants" minibook on pages 28 and 29 for each student. Students cut the pages apart, put them in order, and staple them together on the left side. Read and discuss the material as one more source of information. Complete page 6 of the minibook.

Plants • EMC 858

Name _____

Roots

First Day

Last Day

Can a plant live without roots?   **yes**   **no**

                   Plants • EMC 858

Name _____

Stems

Observe the plants. Color the change you see.

celery

carnation

Write about what you see.

_____

_____

23

Name _____

Leaves Make Food

Circle the things a plant needs to make its own food.

One thing a plant needs to make its own food is not shown. What is it?

orange juice   air   bees

Plants • EMC 858

Name _____

Flowers

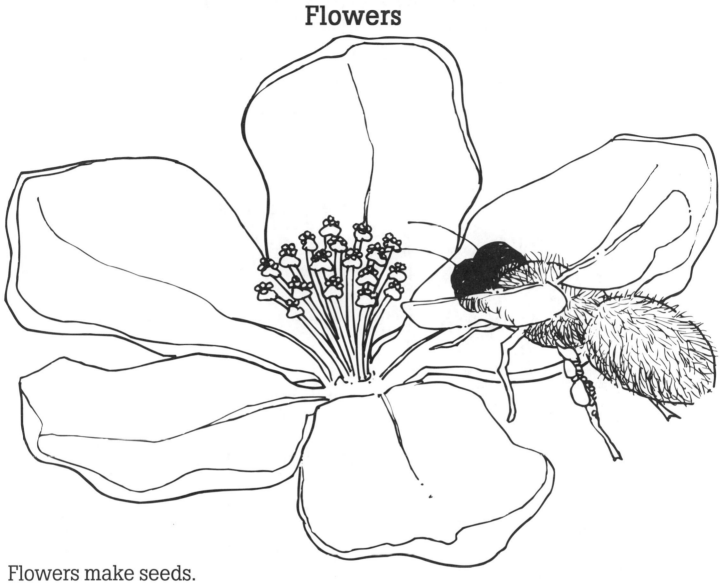

Flowers make seeds.

Plants • EMC 858

Name _____

Each Plant Part Has a Job

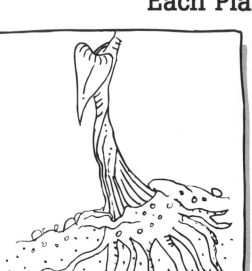

I think a root's job is

_____

_____

I learned that a root's job is

_____

_____

1

- -

Each Plant Part Has a Job

I think a stem's job is

_____

_____

I learned that a stem's job is

_____

_____

2

Each Plant Part Has a Job

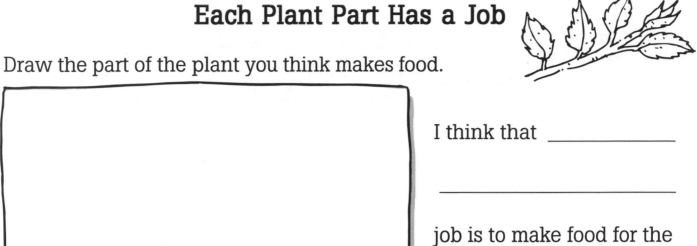

Draw the part of the plant you think makes food.

I think that _____

_____

job is to make food for the plant.

I learned that...

_____

_____

3

- -

Each Plant Part Has a Job

I think a flower's job is

_____

_____

I learned that a flower's job is

_____

_____

4

Flowering Plants

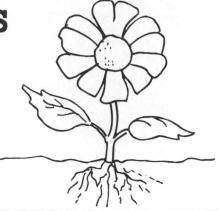

Plants have many parts. Each part has a job to do so the plant can grow.

Roots

Roots hold a plant in place. Roots take the water and minerals from the soil and carry them to the stem where they are carried to the rest of the plant. Some plants store food in the roots.

Here are some roots people eat.

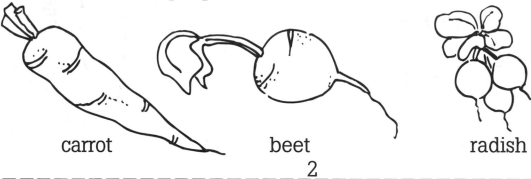

carrot   beet   radish

2

Stems

Stems hold up the leaves and flowers of a plant. Stems have little tubes that carry water and food to the rest of the plant. Grass, flowers, and vines have soft stems. Trees have one hard, wooden stem called a trunk. Most stems grow up toward the sun.

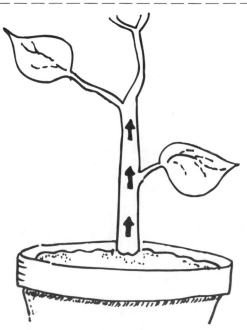

Leaves

A plant can make its own food. The plant uses green cells in the leaves, chlorophyll (klor-o-fil), water from the soil, gas from the air (carbon dioxide), and energy from sunlight to make the food. This is called photosynthesis (fo-to-sin-thuh-sis).

Plants make oxygen (ox-i-jin) for us to breathe.

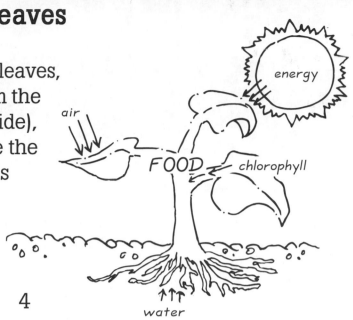

4

Flowers

Flowers are many sizes, colors, and shapes, but they are not just pretty. Flowers make the seeds for the plant. The seeds grow into new plants.

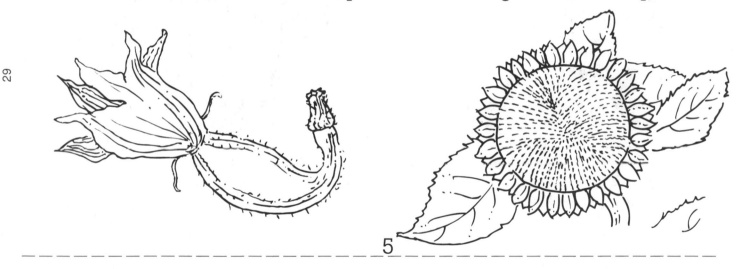

5

Fill in the blanks.

1. Roots take _____ and _____ from the soil to the plant.

2. Roots _____ the plant in place.

3. Plants have _____ that make food.

4. _____ carry water and food around the plant.

5. Flowers make _____.

6. _____ grow into new plants.

The fruit of a flowering plant contains seeds.

What's Inside a Fruit?

- Show the class two kinds of fruit. Ask, "What are these called?" If they answer with the names of the individual fruits, say, "Can you think of one name that tells what these are?" Continue questioning until you get the answer "fruit."

- Then ask students to name other kinds of fruit. Prompt them to continue naming fruit as you create a list on chart paper entitled "Fruit." You will return to the list later to make corrections and additions.

- Cut open both fruits. Ask, "What is inside these pieces of fruit?" Record their observations on a chart for the class logbook entitled "What Is Inside Fruit?"

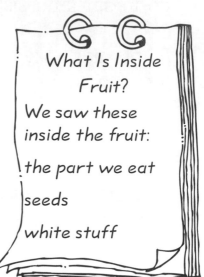

What Is Inside Fruit?
We saw these inside the fruit:
the part we eat
seeds
white stuff

How Many Seeds?

Write the following questions on the chalkboard or an overhead transparency, and ask students to think about them as they do the exploration described below:

"Do all these fruits have seeds?"
"Are the seeds the same in every fruit?"
"Do all the fruits have the same number of seeds?"

Materials

- a whole apple, pear, and orange cut in half for each group
- paper plates
- record form on page 32, reproduced for each student
- plastic spoons
- damp paper towels

Steps to Follow

1. Divide the class into small groups.
2. Give each group a paper plate with all three cut fruits.
3. Provide a plastic spoon for scooping out seeds.
4. Students estimate how many seeds they will find in each whole fruit and record it on their forms.
5. Students count the number of seeds in each type of fruit and record the results.
   (Save the seeds for future use. Put each type in a separate self-closing bag and label it.)

                                           Plants • EMC 858

Graph the Results

- Reproduce the graph on page 33 on an overhead transparency to use with the class as you record the results of their exploration.

- Have each group share their results. Graph the most and least seeds in each type of fruit.

  After completing the graph, ask questions such as:

  "Did all fruits have the same kind and number of seeds inside?"
  "Can you tell how many seeds are inside by looking at the outside of the fruit?"

Is It a Fruit?

- Ask students to write a definition of "fruit." Record their definitions on a page entitled "Fruit Is..." for the class logbook. *(Fruit is the part of the plant that contains the seeds.)* Students can also write the definitions in their individual logs.

- Show the group a banana and a kiwi. Ask, "Do soft fruits like these have seeds?" Cut these open to verify that they do have seeds. Use a magnifying glass for a closer look.

- Refer to the chart entitled "Fruit Is...?" Point to each item on the list and ask, "Is this a fruit? Does it have seeds?" Make corrections and additions.

- Reproduce page 34 for each student. To further assess their understanding of fruit, check answers by examining the 12 foods listed. This page will go into their individual plant logs.

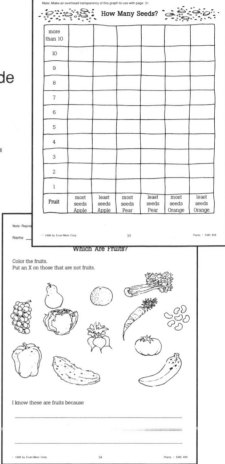

- Extend student understanding of what constitutes "fruit." Have a selection of types of fruit not commonly called fruit — pea pods, rose hips, a squash, a tomato, etc. Through careful questioning, guide students to the understanding that the plant part that contains seeds is a fruit. Return to the class logbook entry "Fruit Is..." to make additions or corrections in the class's definitions.

Seed Search

- Reproduce pages 35 and 36 for each student to accompany this homework activity. They are to collect seeds at home and record information about each seed. Seeds too large to attach to the form can be brought in small plastic bags. When the seed forms are returned, staple them between sheets of construction paper to form a class seed book.

OR

- Display the seeds brought in by students. These may be pinned to a bulletin board or placed on a shelf or a table.

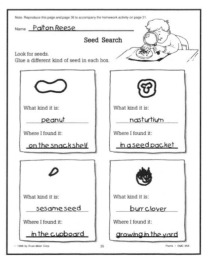

Note: Reproduce this form for each student to use with page 30.

Name _____

How Many Seeds?

Type of Fruit	Apple	Pear	Orange
How many seeds we think there are:			
How many seeds we found:			
Glue a seed here.			

What I learned about fruit and seeds:

_____

_____

_____

Plants • EMC 858

 # How Many Seeds?

Fruit	most seeds Apple	least seeds Apple	most seeds Pear	least seeds Pear	most seeds Orange	least seeds Orange
more than 10						
10						
9						
8						
7						
6						
5						
4						
3						
2						
1						

Name _____

Which Are Fruits?

Color the fruits.
Put an X on those that are not fruits.

I know these are fruits because

_____

_____

_____

34

Name _____

Seed Search

Look for seeds.
Glue a different kind of seed in each box.

What kind it is: _____ Where I found it: _____	What kind it is: _____ Where I found it: _____
What kind it is: _____ Where I found it: _____	What kind it is: _____ Where I found it: _____

Dear Parents,

We are learning about seeds as part of our study of plants. Your child is to find four different seeds to bring to class. The seeds and record sheet are to be returned to school by _____.

Thank you for your help.

P. S. Your kitchen cupboards can be a good source of different types of seeds.

- -

Dear Parents,

We are learning about seeds as part of our study of plants. Your child is to find four different seeds to bring to class. The seeds and record sheet are to be returned to school by _____.

Thank you for your help.

P. S. Your kitchen cupboards can be a good source of different types of seeds.

Seeds contain new plants.

What's in a Seed?

Reproduce the "Inside a Seed" booklet (pages 39–42) for each student.

Follow these steps:

1. Cut out the bean shapes and staple the pages in order, using two staples at the top edge.
2. Students write their names on the first page.
3. Show a handful of lima bean seeds. Generate a discussion by asking, "What do you think is inside these seeds?"
4. Students draw and write an answer on "What I think is inside a seed" (page 1).

The rest of the pages will be completed later.

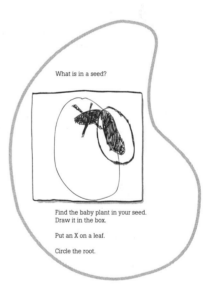

What is in a seed?

Find the baby plant in your seed. Draw it in the box.

Put an X on a leaf.

Circle the root.

Examine Seeds

• Soak the lima bean seeds overnight. Give each student two beans (in case one falls apart before it can be examined) and a small paper plate. Make magnifying glasses available so students can get an up-close look at the parts.

• Students open the seeds carefully to see what is inside. Encourage student interaction as they explore their seeds. Talking about what they see and discussing what each part might be facilitates the learning process.

• Students record their observations on page 2 of their "Inside a Seed" booklets.

     Plants • EMC 858

Are Seeds the Same Inside?

- Extend the exploration of seeds by asking, "Do all seeds have baby plants inside? How can we find out?" If students have difficulty coming up with a plan, use careful questioning to guide them. ("Would it help to look inside other kinds of seeds? What seeds can we use? How shall we set up our experiment?")

Once the plan is established, ask them to predict what they will find. Use some of the larger seeds saved from earlier activities and bring in additional seeds. Peas and corn work well for this exploration. Be sure to soak the seeds overnight before opening.

- Have students record the results of the investigation in their individual logs. Discuss what is common to every seed.

- Make an overhead transparency of page 43, showing a diagram of a seed with the parts labeled to confirm or correct student learnings.

- Ask the students to help you write a definition of a seed. Record it in the class logbook on a page entitled "A Seed." Students should add the definitions to their individual logs.

Plant a Seed

Ask students to explain what will happen if they plant the seeds. Record their conclusions.

Give each student a bean seed to plant. When the seeds have sprouted above the soil, have the students complete page 3 of the "Inside a Seed" booklet.

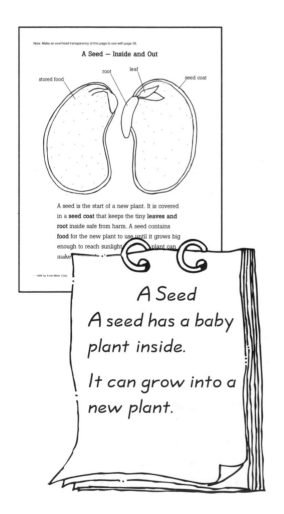

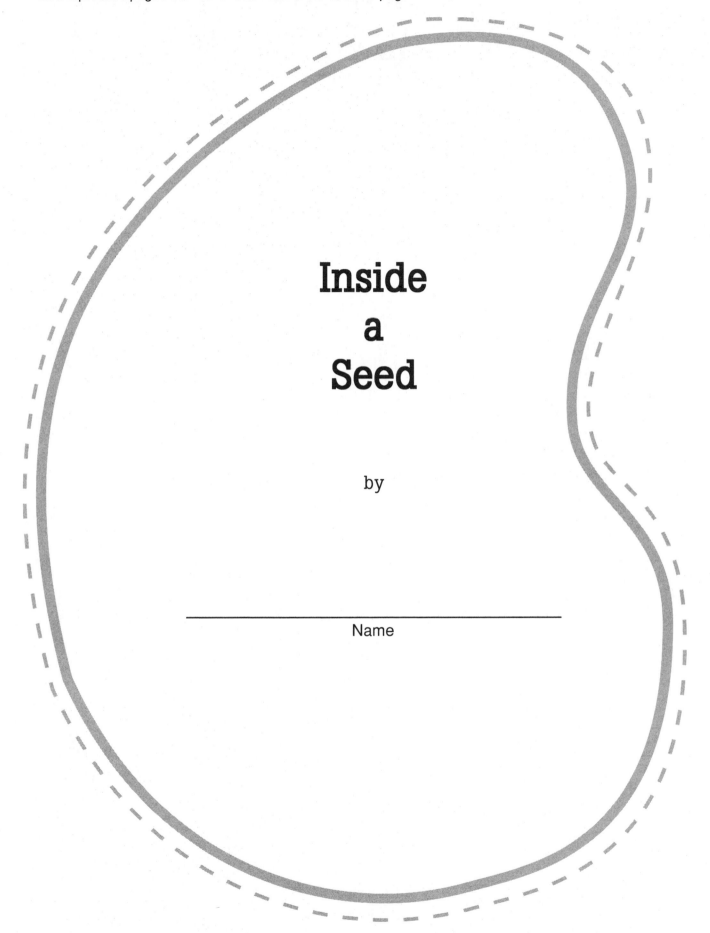

Inside
a
Seed

by

_____
Name

What I think is inside a seed:

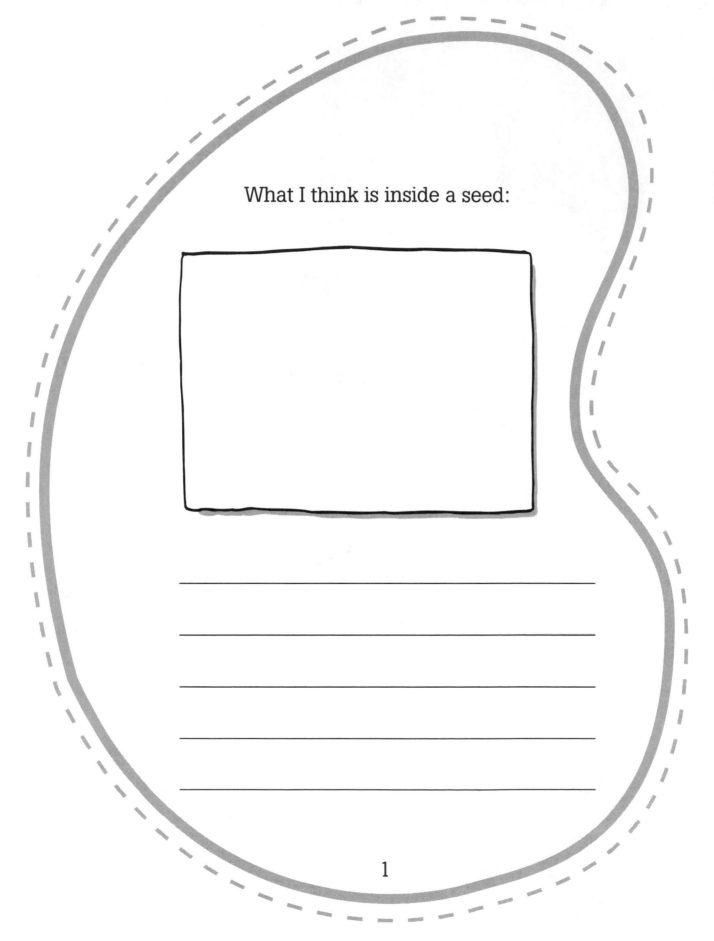

_____

_____

_____

_____

_____

1

Plants • EMC 858

What is in a seed?

Find the baby plant in your seed.
Draw it in the box.

Put an X on a leaf.

Circle the root.

2

What happened after I
planted my seed:

_____
_____
_____
_____

3

A Seed — Inside and Out

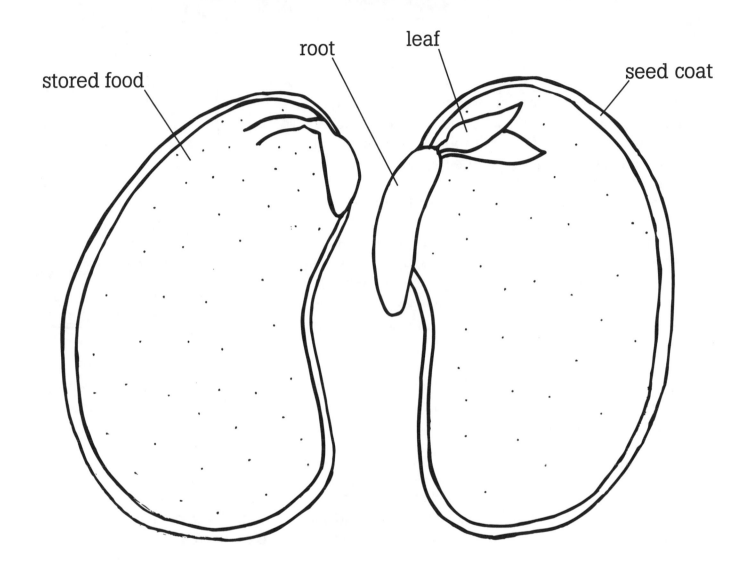

stored food

root

leaf

seed coat

A seed is the start of a new plant. It is covered in a **seed coat** that keeps the tiny **leaves and root** inside safe from harm. A seed contains **food** for the new plant to use until it grows big enough to reach sunlight. Then the plant can make its own food.

Plants • EMC 858

Seeds travel in many ways.

Seeds Travel

- If it is the proper time of year, prepare for this activity by covering your shoes with socks and walking through a field of dry weeds. This should provide you with a good example of seeds that "stick." If Mother Nature has not provided you with appropriate seeds, read *Seeds: Pop, Stick, Glide* by Patricia Lauber (Crown Publishers, 1981) to the class.

    Show the sock (or an appropriate page from the book) and ask students to describe what they see. Ask, "Why do you think some plants have seeds that stick to things?" (*So they can be moved to a new place.*) "Do you know other ways seeds move?" Record their answers on a chart entitled "Seeds Travel."

Seeds Travel

Seeds stick to socks.

Seeds stick to animal fur.

Seeds blow in the wind.

- Check your district audiovisual catalog for a video or filmstrip showing the ways seeds move. After viewing, ask students to recall all the ways the seeds moved. Make additions and corrections to the "Seeds Travel" page of the class logbook.

Collect Samples

- If possible, take the class for a walk through a field or vacant lot. Divide students into groups. Assign a "recorder" to each group. Have students locate seeds and try to determine how the seeds could move. Collect samples of seeds to bring back to the classroom.

- Have each group share what they observed. Record this information in the class logbook.

- Give each student one or more 3" x 5" file cards for mounting the various types of seeds collected. Label each with its name (if known) and how the seed was traveling. If students were unable to collect seeds, review the seeds in *Seeds: Pop, Stick, Glide* and have them draw pictures of the way those seeds travel.

Burr on my do[g]

Maple

Acorn on the ground

Dandelion floating in air

    Post the seed forms or illustrations on a bulletin board entitled "Seeds Move in Many Ways."

Ways Seeds Travel

• Read *The Tiny Seed* by Eric Carle (Scholastic, 1987) to verify ways plants move.

• Provide a collection of seed pods and seeds that might be moved in one or more ways (a coconut that floats, some seeds with "stickers" or "hooks," an acorn or berries that an animal might spread, a maple seed or dandelion seed with "wings," etc.).

List the ways seeds move. Have students examine the seeds you provided and sort them into categories by means of movement. Use this as a time to verify or correct what they have learned about seed movement.

• Reproduce the pictures on pages 46 and 47. Show one picture at a time and have students decide how the seed is traveling. Encourage the use of descriptive words about the seed and its motion (*This seed has sharp hooks. It can stick to a dog's fur. This seed has wings like a helicopter. It can fly in the wind.*).

• Return to the "Seeds Travel" page of the class logbook and make corrections and additions. Then give each student a copy of the minibook on pages 48 and 49. Read the minibook together and have students complete the final page.

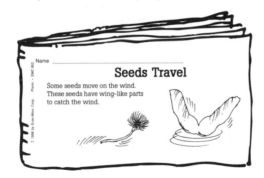

Name _____

Seeds Travel

Some seeds move on the wind.
These seeds have wing-like parts
to catch the wind.

Extension Activity

Invite a farmer or professional gardener to speak to the class about the ways seeds are acquired and how they are used. Students record what they learn in their individual logs.

© 1998 by Evan-Moor Corp.   45   Plants • EMC 858

Plants • EMC 858

Note: Reproduce these cards to use with the activity on page 45.

 Plants • EMC 858

Name _____

Seeds Travel

Some seeds move on the wind.
These seeds have wing-like parts
to catch the wind.

1

Some seeds have hooks or stickers.
These seeds catch in the fur of animals.
The seeds fall off in a new place later.

2

Some plants have seed pods that pop open. The seeds are then
scattered about.

3

Some kinds of birds and bats eat fruit. The seeds of the fruit are carried to new places in the animal's droppings.

4

Some seeds float on water to a new place.

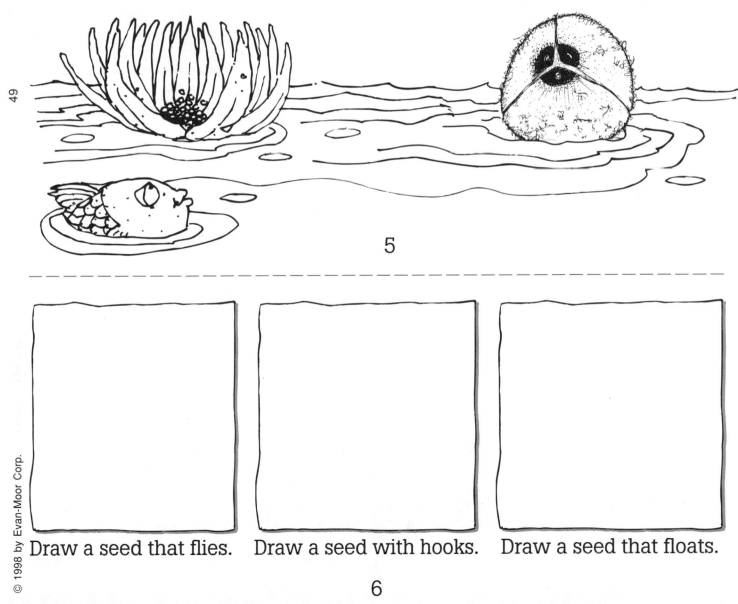

5

Draw a seed that flies.   Draw a seed with hooks.   Draw a seed that floats.

6

Plants change as they grow.

The Plant Growth Cycle

Read *The Seasons of Arnold's Apple Tree* by Gail Gibbons (Harcourt Brace Jovanovich, 1984). Ask students to describe the changes that happen in the story. Record these changes in the class plant log on a page entitled "An Apple Tree."

Have students fold a sheet of paper into fourths, and then draw and write about changes occurring to the plant in the story. Older or more able students may use both sides of the paper to include greater detail about the growth cycle. Have them put the page in their individual plant logs.

An Apple Tree

The apple tree got bigger.

Leaves grew on the tree.

Flowers grew on the tree.

Apples grew on the tree.

Seed-Growing Bags

Prepare plastic growing bags with your students.

Materials (per student)

- 1-quart, self-closing plastic bag
- 2 white paper towels
- 4 bean seeds
- masking tape or pins
- permanent marking pen
- Growing Bag Log on page 53, reproduced for each student

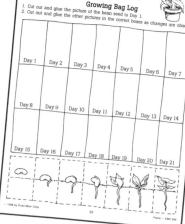

Steps to Follow

1. Fold the paper towels and place in the bag. (They should touch the bottom of the bag.)
2. Draw a line across the bag about two inches (5 cm) from the bottom. (Write student's name on the bag with permanent marking pen.)
3. Staple through the bag and towels along the line. (This keeps the seeds from dropping to the bottom of the bag.)
4. Drop the seeds into the bag. Move them until they are evenly spaced.
5. Add water to dampen the towels. (Keep damp, not wet, by adding water as needed.) Zip the bag shut.
6. Tape or pin the growing bag up in the classroom where it will receive sunlight. (Not in direct sunlight as the seeds may burn.)
7. Have students observe the bag each day and record any changes they observe on the Growing Bag Log.

Follow-Up

- Extend the activity by having students measure the growth of a seed. Record the information on a graph on a chart or a bulletin board.

Measure the height of the same plant every day.
Draw a green line to show the height of the plant.

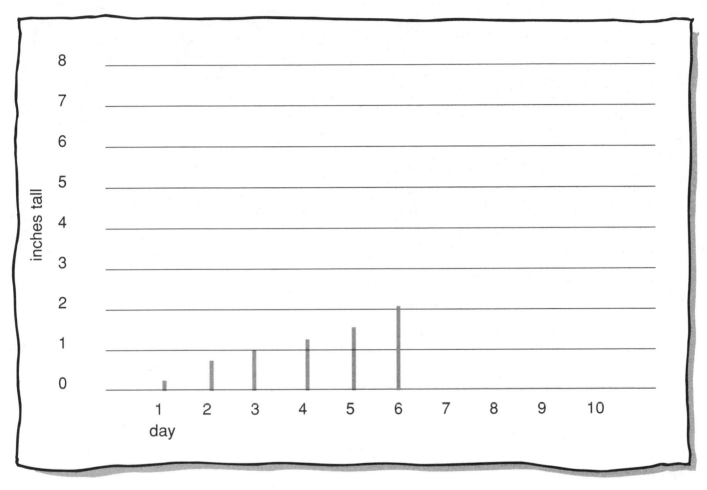

- With students looking at their Growing Bag Logs, discuss the progress made by their bean seeds. Ask, "What happened to your seed on day 4? On which day did leaves open up on your plant? Did all of the seeds grow in the same way? Did they all grow at about the same speed? Did you see a pattern in how the seedlings grew?" Record these observations on a page entitled "Seeds Grow" for the class logbook. Students write what they have learned in their individual logbooks.

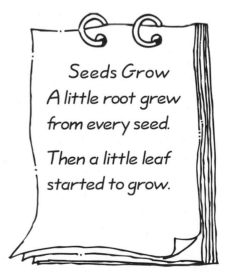

Seeds Grow
*A little root grew
from every seed.*

*Then a little leaf
started to grow.*

Observe Plant Growth

Plant peas in a large container. Place in a sunny area and observe through an entire life cycle.

Materials

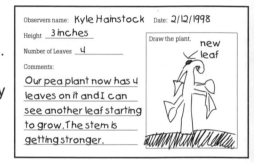

- Several copies of the plant log on page 54, stapled together for each student
- ruler
- soil
- large pot (12" diameter or larger)
- package of pea seeds
  (Soak the seeds overnight before planting.)

Steps to Follow

1. Plant the seeds following directions on the seed package.
2. Observe the plants every day. Measure and record what is seen.
3. After the plant has produced pea pods, discuss what students have learned from observing the cycle. Refer to the records they have kept.

Follow-up

- Have students help write a definition of "life cycle" to go on a page entitled "A Plant Life Cycle" for the class logbook.

- Reproduce the minibook on pages 55 and 56. Students write what they have learned about the stages of the life cycle shown in the book.

Extension Activity

Follow the growth of a garden by reading a story such as *Jack's Garden* by Henry Cole (Greenwillow, 1995).

Then plant an outside vegetable garden in the ground or in large pots. If space is very limited, plant a "salad garden" in pots in the classroom. Also plant fast-growing flowers. This will give students the opportunity to see the changes that occur throughout the life cycle of various types of plants. It will also reinforce the concept that plants grow at different speeds.

Plants • EMC 858

Name _____

Growing Bag Log

1. Cut out and glue the picture of the bean seed to Day 1.
2. Cut out and glue the other pictures in the correct boxes as changes are observed.

Day 1	Day 2	Day 3	Day 4	Day 5	Day 6	Day 7
Day 8	Day 9	Day 10	Day 11	Day 12	Day 13	Day 14
Day 15	Day 16	Day 17	Day 18	Day 19	Day 20	Day 21

Plants • EMC 858

Observer's name: _____ Date: _____

Height _____

Number of Leaves _____

Comments:

_____

_____

_____

_____

_____

Draw the plant.

Observer's name: _____ Date: _____

Height _____

Number of Leaves _____

Comments:

_____

_____

_____

_____

_____

Draw the plant.

Life Cycle of a Pea Plant

by

_____

_____

_____

_____

_____

_____

_____

_____

_____

_____

_____

_____

_____

_____

_____

_____

_____

_____

_____

© 1998 by Evan-Moor Corp.

_____

_____

_____

_____

_____

© 1998 by Evan-Moor Corp.

_____

_____

_____

_____

_____

Plants need food, water, and light to grow.

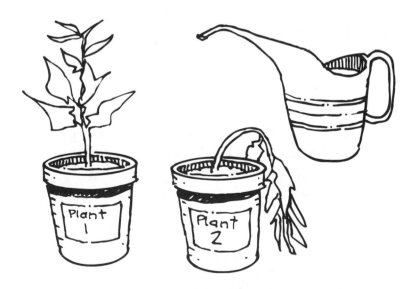

What Do Plants Need?

Bring in a dead plant. Have students observe the plant. Ask, "What do you suppose this plant needed that it didn't get?"

Record their observations in the class plant log on a page entitled "What Plants Need."

What Plants Need
food
water
sunshine
good care

Plants Need Water

This investigation helps students see why plants need water. Students will record observations in a booklet created from pages 61 and 62.

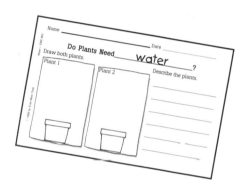

Materials

- record forms on pages 61 and 62; each student will need 3 copies of page 61 and 1 of page 62
- 2 small plants (same type, same size)
- watering can and water

Steps to Follow

1. Ask, "Why do we have to water our plants? What will happen if we don't water for one day? For a lot of days?" Explain that this investigation will help answer those questions.
2. Number the plants 1 and 2.
3. Put the plants in a sunny window.
4. Water plant 1 when soil is dry on the top. DO NOT water plant 2.
5. Have students observe the plants once a week for three weeks and record what they see. When a clear conclusion can be drawn, have the students complete the last page of the observation booklet.

Plants • EMC 858

Plants Need Leaves

This investigation shows what happens if a green plant is missing too many of its food-producing leaves. Students will record observations in a minibook created from pages 61 and 62.

Materials

- two plants (same type, size, condition)
- record forms on pages 61 and 62; each student will need 4 copies of page 61 and 1 of page 62
- pencil

Steps to Follow

1. Prior to doing the experiment, review with students how plants get their food (page 19).
2. Number the plants 1 and 2.
3. Remove all but two or three leaves from plant 2. If new leaves grow, remove them.
4. Place both plants in the sunlight. Give each plant the same care.
5. Have students observe weekly and record the changes seen over a period of time (at least once a month).

Plants Need Sunlight

This investigation shows that green plants need sunlight.

Materials

- record sheet on page 63, reproduced for each student
- 2 small plants (same type, same size)
- a brown paper bag

Steps to Follow

1. Ask, "Why is it important for a plant to get sunlight? What will happen if a plant doesn't get enough sunlight for a lot of days?" Explain that this investigation will help answer those questions.
2. Number the plants 1 and 2.
3. Put the plants in a sunny window. Cover plant 2 with a bag.
4. Water each plant as needed, but always keep the one plant under its bag.
5. Observe the plant once a week for four weeks, and have students record what they see.

Plants Need Soil

This investigation shows that the kind of soil can affect the way a plant grows.

Materials

- three types of soil
  (sandy, clay, soil from under a tree, or potting soil from nursery)
- a package of seeds (radish, nasturtiums, or other quick-growing plant)
- trowel or large spoon
- a pot for each type of soil
- water
- labels for pots (naming type of soil)
- record form on page 64, reproduced for each student

Steps to Follow

1. Show various types of soil. Ask, "What is different about these soils? Will plants grow the same in each one? Which soil do you think will be best? Why?"
2. Fill each pot with a different soil. Number and label the pots with the soil type.
3. Soak the seeds overnight.
4. Plant several seeds in each pot.
5. Set the pots in a sunny location. Water as needed.
6. Observe the plants for a number of weeks. Then have the students complete the record form.

Summary Activities

Plant Minibook

Reproduce pages 65 and 66 for each student. Cut apart and staple to form a six-page minibook. Read and complete the minibook to confirm what has been learned.

Write a Healthy Plant Guide

Have the class write *A Guide to Growing Healthy Plants*.

1. Make a list of the plant needs to be covered in the guide. These will form the "chapters" in the guide.

   List additional material they want to include in the book (gardening tools, a list of easy-to-grow plants, etc.).

2. Make a list of each page that will be included in the guide. The guide might contain:

   front cover
   Table of Contents
   Introduction
   Soil
   Water
   Sunlight
   Tools
   Easy-to-Grow Plants
   back cover

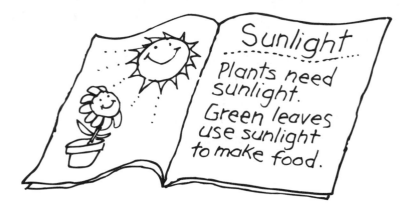

3. Assign each part of the guide to a group of students. They will be responsible for writing and illustrating their page. Allow time for rough drafts to be written and shared with the class and for revisions to be made.

4. Have students write the final text and draw illustrations on chart paper. Bind the pages inside the cover.

5. Keyboard the text on the computer to make a copy for each student to take home.

Community Resources

Invite speakers (nursery worker, farmer, etc.) to talk about how they meet the needs of their crops. Then take a field trip to a nursery and/or a local farm to see this firsthand.

When you return to school, discuss what was learned. Record observations in the class logbook on a page entitled "Plants Need...". Reproduce page 67 for each student. They are to draw and write about what was learned on the field trip.

Name _____ Date _____

Do Plants Need_____?

Draw both plants.   Describe the plants.

Plant 1    Plant 2

_____

_____

_____

_____

_____

_____

_____

- -

Name _____ Date _____

Do Plants Need_____?

Draw both plants.   Describe the plants.

Plant 1    Plant 2

_____

_____

_____

_____

_____

Name _____ Date _____

Which plant grew better?   Plant 1   Plant 2

What I learned: _____

_____

_____

_____

_____

- -

Name _____ Date _____

Which plant grew better?   Plant 1   Plant 2

What I learned: _____

_____

_____

_____

Name _____

Do Plants Need Sunlight?

Draw or write what you see.

After 1 week:	After 2 weeks:
Plant 1 Plant 2	Plant 1 Plant 2

After 3 weeks:	After 4 weeks:
Plant 1 Plant 2	Plant 1 Plant 2

Which plant grew better? _____

What I learned about plants and sunlight: _____

_____

Name _____

Which Soil Is Best?

We planted seeds in three kinds of soil.
This is what I saw after the plants grew.

Draw the plants here.

soil 1: _____   soil 2: _____   soil 3: _____

What I learned: _____

_____

_____

_____

Name _____

What Do Plants Need To Grow?

Plants are like people. They need a
good place to live. The soil must be right.
They must have food and air. They must
have the right amount of water and sunshine.

1

Plants have special green cells (chlorophyll) that can make food.
These cells are in the plant's leaves.

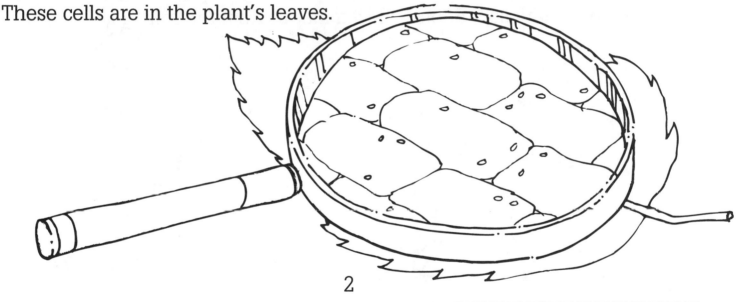

2

Roots collect water from the soil. The
roots carry the water to the stem. Tiny
tubes in the stem carry the water up to
the leaves.

Water is used to help the leaves make
food for the plant. Water is needed to
help seeds begin to grow.

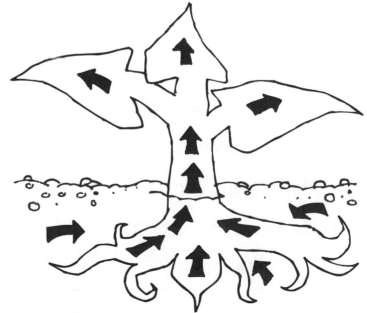

3

The right amount of sunlight is needed for a plant to grow. The leaves of a plant take energy from the sunlight. They use it to help make food for the plant.

Different plants need different amounts of sunlight. Some plants like to be out in the hot sun. Other plants need to be in shady places.

I MAKE MY OWN FOOD

4

Different plants like different kinds of soil. Some grow best in sandy soil. Some like rich, dark soil. Roots collect minerals from the soil.

5

Fill in the missing words.

1. Roots take _____ from the soil. They carry it up into the plant.

2. Plants use energy from _____ to help make food.

3. Green leaves make _____ for the whole plant.

4. Plants get the gas carbon dioxide out of the _____.

5. Plants need the right kind of _____ to grow in.

sunshine	air	soil	food	water

6

Note: Reproduce this form for each student to use with page 60.

Name ____

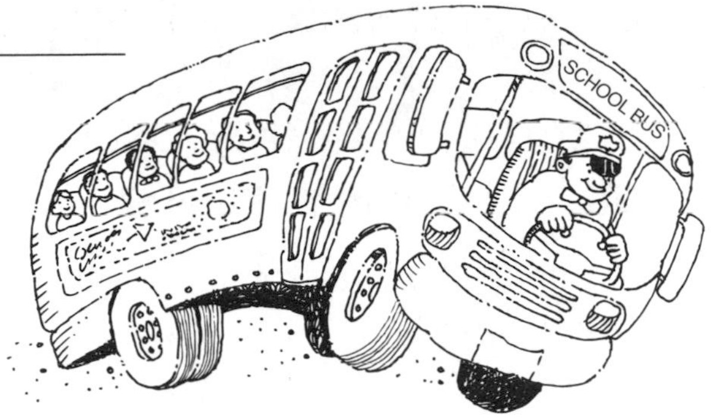

Field Trip

We went on a trip to _______________.

This is what I saw:

This is what I learned: ______________________________________

____

____

____

____

People need plants for food and oxygen.

What Comes from Plants?

Searching the Classroom

Challenge students to find other things in the classroom that originally came from a plant. Have a few obvious things around the room — a bouquet of flowers, a piece of fruit, something made of wood — to get students started. Give students five minutes to explore the room, then call them together to compile a list of the items they discovered for the class logbook.

Searching at Home

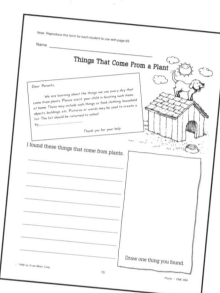

• Reproduce page 70 as a homework activity. Students will draw, cut and paste, or write a list of items they find at home that come from plants.

After students return their homework forms, have a sharing time where each child shares one item from his or her list. Confirm or correct understandings as appropriate.

Record the names of items in the following categories in the class logbook — things we eat, things we wear, things we use. Have students illustrate the items and display them on a bulletin board.

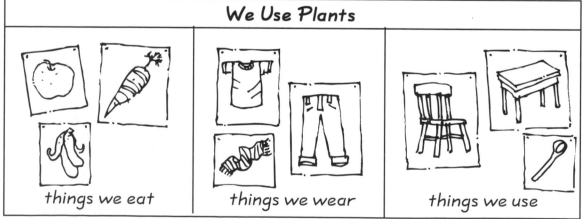

We Use Plants

things we eat · things we wear · things we use

Follow-Up

• Read the sections from *The Reason for a Flower* by Ruth Heller that describe everyday items that come from plants.
• Check your district audio-visual catalog to locate appropriate videos, films, or filmstrips to show manufacturing from plant to finished product.
• If possible, visit a lumber mill or a factory that makes cloth so students can see firsthand the process of using plants to create something we use.

Plants Make Oxygen

One of the most important products provided by plants will probably go unmentioned — oxygen. Do the following demonstration to show that plants make a special gas we use.

Materials

- green water plant
- large, clear glass jar
- clear plastic funnel
- test tube
- water

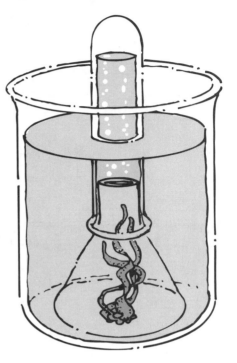

Steps to Follow:

1. Fill the jar with water. Place the water plant on the bottom of the jar and cover it with the funnel.
2. Fill the test tube with water. Hold your thumb over the open end to keep from spilling the water. Turn it upside down and lower the open end of the tube into the jar. Fit it over the narrow end of the funnel.
3. Place the jar in the sunlight. Have students observe the jar periodically. After a while they will see tiny bubbles of gas from the plant begin to gather at the top of the test tube. The gas will begin to push the water out.

Explain that the gas being made is oxygen. People and animals take in oxygen when they breathe. We need oxygen to live. Help them understand that all green plants release oxygen. (Oxygen is produced as a by-product of photosynthesis.)

Summary Activities

- Ask students to explain how people and animals depend on plants. Record their conclusions in the class logbook on a page entitled "We Use Plants." Have students write in their individual logs as well.

- Reproduce page 71 to extend student understanding of the wide range of items we use that come from plants.

- Reproduce and compile the minibook on pages 72 and 73. Have students read the information and complete the activity on the last page.

- Engage older students in a discussion of what would happen to people and to animals if there were suddenly no more plants on Earth. This is a good place to read a book about rainforests and discuss their vital role in Earth's ecosystem.

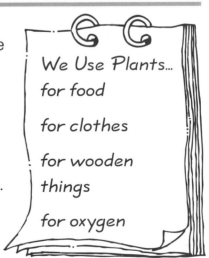

We Use Plants...
for food
for clothes
for wooden things
for oxygen

Note: Reproduce this form for each student to use with page 68.

Name _____

Things That Come from a Plant

Dear Parents,

We are learning about the things we use every day that come from plants. Please assist your child in locating several items at home. These may include things such as food, clothing, household objects, buildings, etc. Pictures or words may be used to create a list. The list should be returned to school by_____.

Thank you for your help.

I found these things that come from plants.

_____

_____

_____

_____

_____

_____

_____

Draw one thing you found.

Plants • EMC 858

Name _____

We Need Plants

Find the things we use that come from plants.

```
v e g e t a b l e s b
r c o r k l u m b e r
u f o o d p a p e r e
b o o x y g e n r p a
b o x c e r e a l e d
e f u r n i t u r e o
r n c l o t h i n g i
m e d i c i n e o i l
f r u i t f a b r i c
```

Word Box

bread	dye	furniture	paper
cereal	fabric	lumber	rubber
clothing	food	medicine	vegetables
cork	fruit	oxygen	

Name _____

People and Animals Need Plants

The oxygen people and animals breathe comes from plants. When a leaf makes food for the plant, it gives off a gas. That gas is oxygen.

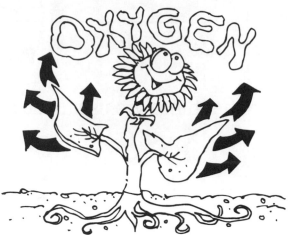

1

Both people and animals eat plants. We eat their leaves, roots, and stems. We eat their fruits and seeds.

2

We don't just eat plants. We use the wood from trees (lumber) to build houses, barns, fences, and furniture. We use parts of trees to make paper of all kinds.

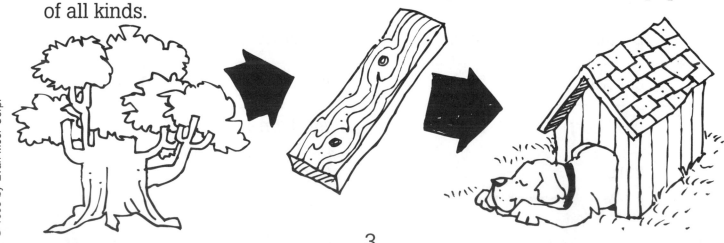

3

72

Some kinds of material are made from plants. This material is used to make clothing and other things we use.

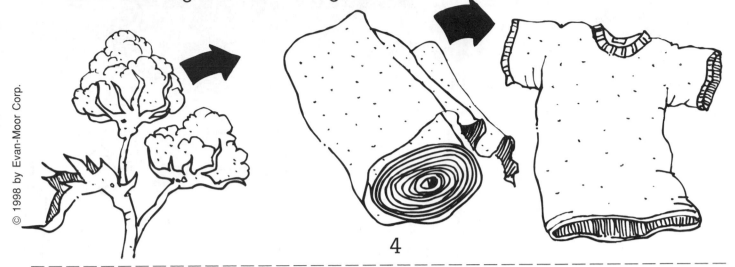

4

Plants are used in other ways, too. Gum comes from tree sap. Colorful dyes come from plants. Many kinds of medicines come from plants.

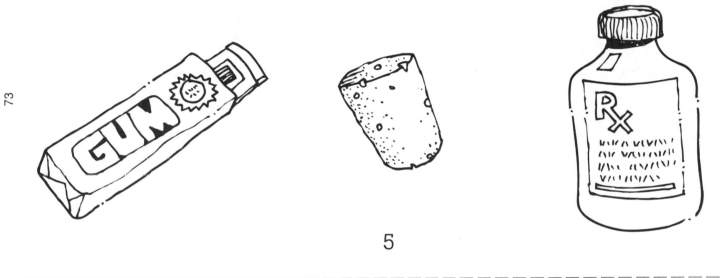

5

Draw something you use that comes from a plant.

CONCEPT
Not all plants reproduce from seeds made by flowers.

Plants That Never Bloom

- Read *Plants That Never Ever Bloom* by Ruth Heller (Grosset, 1984). Ask, "What can you tell me about the plants in this book?" Record their information on a class logbook page entitled "Plants That Don't Bloom."

- If reasonable, walk around the school to look for examples of plants described in the story. Have students take clipboards with paper and pencils to draw what they find.

- Reproduce the minibook on pages 76 and 77 for each student. Read the book together and have students complete the final page.

- Divide the class into small groups. Give each group a pine cone, a fern with spore cases, a mushroom, and a magnifying glass. Have them try to locate the parts that could grow into new plants.

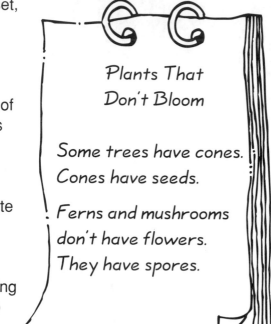

Plants That Don't Bloom

Some trees have cones.
Cones have seeds.

Ferns and mushrooms don't have flowers.
They have spores.

Categorizing Plants

1. Reproduce a set of the pictures on pages 76–78 for each group. Cut the pictures apart and mix them up.
2. First have students separate the pictures into two sets — plants with seeds; plants with spores (no seeds).
3. Next have them separate the set of plants with seeds into two groups — flowering plants; plants with cones.
4. Finally, have them separate the seedless plants into two groups — ferns; mushrooms.
5. Have students explain how each of the four sets of plants will grow new plants. Correct any misconceptions at this time.
6. Update the information in the class plant log. Students may also write in their individual logs.

Mushroom Prints

Materials

- mushroom caps
  (mature with open gills)
- construction paper
  (white if using brown mushrooms,
  dark if using white mushrooms)

Steps to Follow

1. Carefully remove the stem from the mushroom.
2. Place the mushroom cap gill side down on construction paper.
3. Let the mushroom sit for two days.
4. Lift the mushroom cap to see the spore print underneath.

Fern Prints

Materials

- fern fronds with spore cases
- construction paper
- tempera paint
- paintbrushes
- newspaper

Steps to Follow

1. Thin the tempera paint with a little water.
2. Place newspapers on the work area.
3. Lay the fern on the newspaper with the spore cases facing up. Brush tempera over the fern frond.
4. Lay the construction paper on top of the fern. Press gently (don't rub) over the surface.
5. Lift the construction paper to see the fern print.

Plants • EMC 858

Note: Reproduce these cards to use with the activity on page 74.

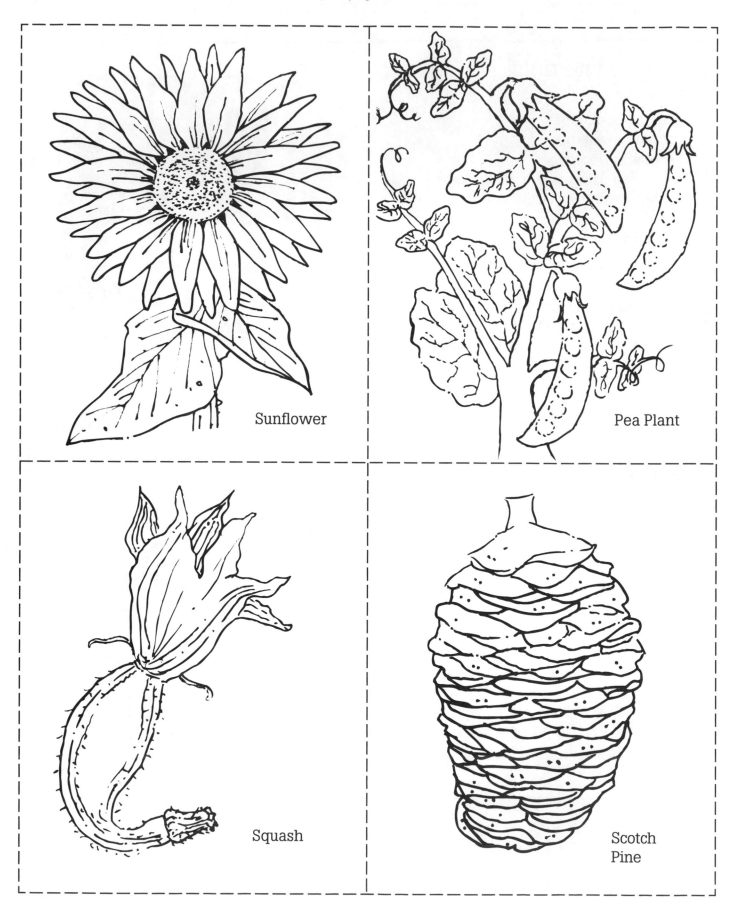

Sunflower

Pea Plant

Squash

Scotch
Pine

Plants • EMC 858

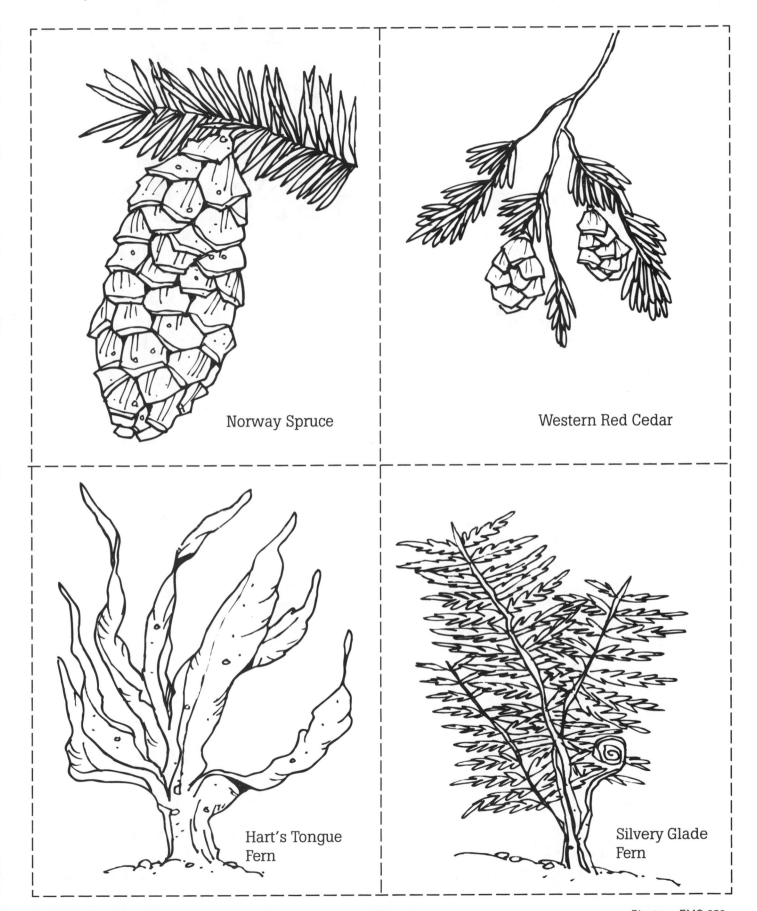

Norway Spruce

Western Red Cedar

Hart's Tongue
Fern

Silvery Glade
Fern

Note: Reproduce these cards to use with the activity on page 74.

Lady Fern

Pine Mushroom

Parasol Mushroom

Bay Gyromitra

Plants with No Flowers

Some plants grow from seeds.
Some plants grow from spores.

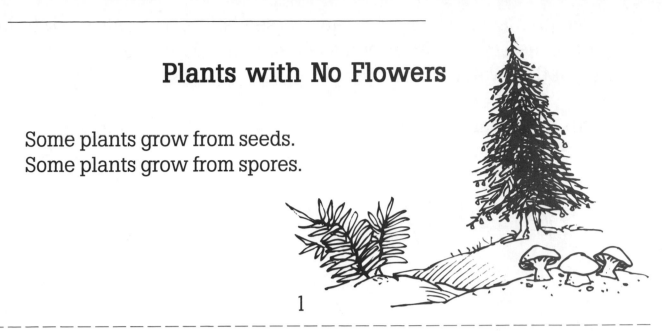

1

Some plants have no flowers but still grow from seeds. These plants have a cone to hold the seeds. The cone has hard scales that protect the seeds until they are ripe.

The seeds are carried by the wind when they fall from the cones.

seeds

2

Inside of a pine cone

Cones do not all look alike. They come in all sizes and shapes. They do not all drop their seeds in the same way either.

Cypress Cone

White Pine Cone

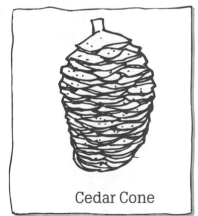

Cedar Cone

3

Some plants have no flowers and no seeds. These plants grow from tiny parts called spores. The spores fall from the plant and are carried away by wind or water. When the spores land, new plants begin to grow.

Ferns and mushrooms are two of the land plants that grow from spores.

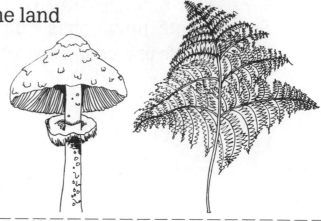

4

Seaweeds live in the salty ocean. They grow from spores. Seaweeds can be red, green, or brown. The leaves make food for the plant. Some seaweeds are small. Others are as tall as trees.

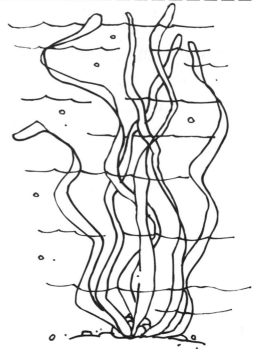

5

Box the fern.
Circle the mushroom.
Cross out the seaweed.
Color the plants that have spores.

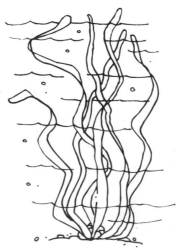
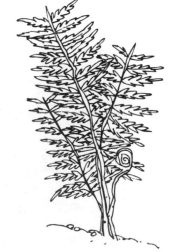

6